ÉMILE JADOUL

My First Year

Stick a picture of me here ↗

This book belongs to...
CLAUDIA AMÉLIE

Capella

Love Auntie Teresa
& Uncle Dan
2012

...a baby coming soon!

Mummy said:

Daddy said:

My first pictures

They thought about me for 9 months, week after week.

Daddy said I would be:
a little princess, a bold knight...

Mummy thought I would be:
a little prince, a little madam...

Meanwhile,
daddy and mummy got ready for my arrival.

This is my bedroom...

Daddy moved his sofa, tv + computer downstairs, and Baba + Gigi helped to wash the walls during their visit in February 2012.

...and these are my first pyjamas!

These were given to us as a hand-me-down from Katherine, plus some from the kids swap... Thank goodness we had a tiny tiny pair to fit you (by Gagou).

Thinking of my name!

Mummy and daddy looked for boys' names:

Henrik

Eric

Matteo

Stefan

Frank

Paul

Ivan

...and girls' names:

Claudia

Francesca

Phillipa

Brigitte

Isabella

Natalia

Yvette

...ssh, it's a secret!

Other things they thought about...

A family

Will I look like my daddy?

Here is my daddy

Or

resemblance?

Will I look like my mummy?

like...

Here is my mummy

Here I am!

Hurry up!

At last, the big day arrived: mummy was ready. So was daddy. She said: "Quick, we'd better go!"

Date April 25, 2012
Time we left ~ 1:45 AM
Hospital Lions Gate Hospital

From the time I left the bedroom, to the emergency at the hospital, Mommy had 4 contractions! One in the living room, in the car before we left, one in the car at the Emergency + one in the hospital hallway! Doula Jill Culpitts was with me in the back seat while Daddy drove ever so slowly yet quickly as Mommy was going "Owe, Owe"!

On the day...

Was it night time? Was it day time?
Was it warm? Was it cold?

And here I am!

Date _APRIL 25, 2012_ (ANZAC DAY IN AUSTRALIA, NZ)
Time _____
My birth sign _TAURUS_
Day of the week _WEDNESDAY_

Princess or Knight?

Daddy and mummy call me: my little angel, ------

But my real name is:
CLAUDIA AMELIE

Daddy and mummy announced my arrival...

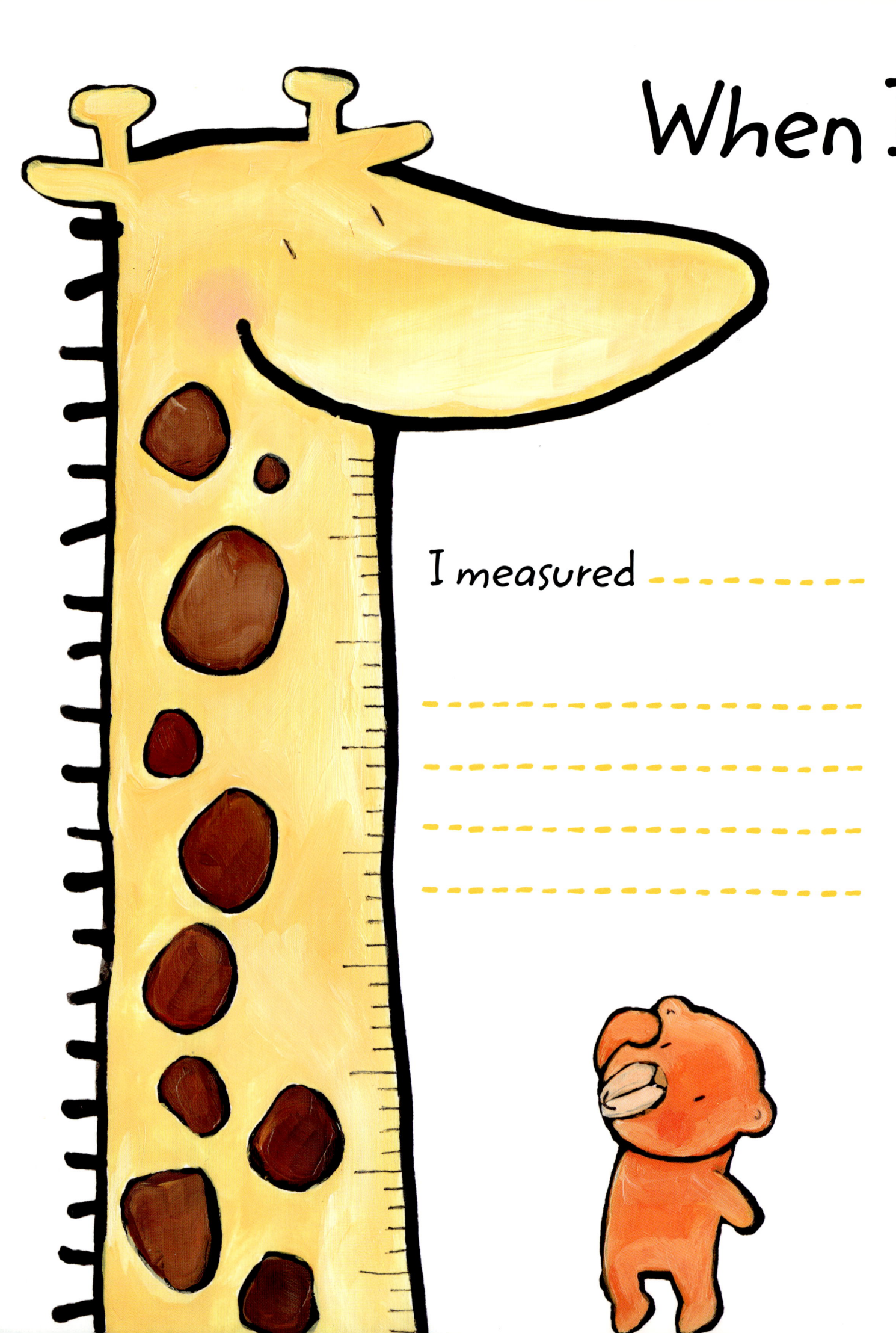

was born...

I weighed _7 lbs even!_

My hair was _____

My eyes were _DARK BLUE_

My first cuddle

My first kiss

Welcome!

Everybody welcomed me...

My first presents

My cuddly toy and me

That year...

In the world

Little things I used to do

My home

Splash!
It's bathtime...

Yummy!
It's dinnertime!

Beddy byes!

My first ever whole night's sleep _____
Do I suck my thumb? _____
Do I have a dummy? _____
I wake up every _____ hours.

In my bed, there is _____
_____

My favourite nursery rhyme is _____

_____
_____
_____

My first smile

The first face I pulled

I am one!

My presents ------------------------

Who was there? --------------------

I can walk

on all fours...

on two feet...

I'm growing up

I look like my dad when I

I look like my mum when I -----------------

My first words

I call my mum ------------------------
I call my dad -------------------------

When I'm hungry, I say ---------------
When I'm thirsty, I say ----------------

Other little words ---------------------

My first little accident

Other things about me